CHARISMA MADE EASY

Simple Steps to Being More Charismatic & Likable

Darcy Carter

FREE GIFT

Struggling in Social Situations?

Get 5 Quick Fixes to Boost Your Confidence

FREE DOWNLOAD

⬇ ⬇ ⬇

https://subscribepage.com/charisma

CONTENTS

INTRODUCTION

Have you ever wished you could walk into any place at any time and instantly attract the people there to you? Imagine being a person who effortlessly navigates social situations. Who communicates with confidence and ease. The person who others are naturally drawn to. Picture yourself at a party or an event at work. Imagine how people gravitate towards you, eager to engage in conversation, captivated by your presence. You become the person who lights up the room, leaving a lasting impression wherever you go.

Charisma has the power to open doors and create opportunities you never thought possible. Not only that, it helps you build meaningful relationships and leave a lasting impression. Charisma, simply put, is a personal magnetism that gives you **the ability to attract and influence** other people. Charismatic people effortlessly express themselves in any situation. Charismatic people are naturally magnetic, drawing others toward them both personally and professionally. Those in their presence are impressed by their confidence and authenticity, which leave a lasting impression. They make them feel comfortable, valued, and genuinely understood. Naturally, they want to meet with them again.

Many people assume that charisma is a mysterious quality. You either have it or you don't. Perhaps you think that charisma is reserved only for extroverts, but that's simply not true. Charismatic people aren't necessarily the loudest or most outgoing in the room. In fact, some of the most charismatic individuals are quiet and introverted. For those personality types, charisma comes from their ability to listen intently and connect deeply with others on a personal level.

For example, here are two very different kinds of charismatic people.

- *Eckhart Tolle:* His charisma is characterized by his calm, reflective speaking style. His gentle demeanor, thoughtful pauses, and profound insights draw people in. His charisma creates a peaceful and introspective atmosphere.

- *Tony Robbins:* His charisma lies in his high energy and motivational speaking style. He uses his physical presence, dynamic gestures, and powerful voice to create a sense of urgency and empowerment.

<u>Charisma is not an inherent trait that only a select few possess.</u> No, it's a skill that anyone can develop with the right knowledge and practice. We are **all** born with the potential to be charismatic and likable. However, along life's journey, we have been socialized and stigmatized "Don't do this, don't do that. You're not this, you're not that." Such statements force us into shells and damage our charisma. But I'm telling you, you can develop charisma and enhance what's already there.

Maybe you've experienced the sting of loneliness or the frustration of missed opportunities to connect with others. Instead of facing those situations with more shyness, nervousness, and anxiety, imagine a different reality. No more missed chances, no more nights spent alone, and no more connections slipping away. By developing charisma, you can transform these painful experiences into moments of confidence and connection. This book will show you how to reclaim and enhance your natural charisma. It is your guide to unlocking the secrets of charisma and becoming a more likable person.

But who am I to teach you about becoming more charismatic and likable? My name is Darcy Carter, and I'm an established author of various books on social skills. But my knowledge goes beyond books. It comes from real-world testing and experience. I've lived in some of the biggest cities in the world, making friends and connections everywhere.

Charisma was my secret weapon.

I developed it while working in nightclubs, practicing in the streets, and engaging in random conversations in shops, restaurants, malls, and networking events—you name it. It hasn't always been easy. I've faced awkward moments and learned through trial and error. Through this journey, I've learned how to become more charismatic and likable. I hope you are able to enjoy and integrate the insights I've decided to share with you here.

Many books have a few great ideas that could be explained much more concisely. This book is designed to be concise and practical. Getting to the point fast and definitively is my goal. You see, charisma is developed through action, not just reading. Think of it like building muscle; you need to do the exercises to see the results. This book will give you the knowledge, but **you need to go out and practice what you learn.**

I will guide you through the process of overcoming social anxiety and unlocking your full, charismatic potential. Whether you're aiming to enrich your social life, advance in your career, or simply feel more comfortable in your own skin. By following the actionable steps and exercises provided, you'll become a more charismatic and likable person who stands out in a positive way. You will learn practical steps and exercises to enhance your **presence**, **warmth**, and **power**. These are the three core elements of charisma that we will explore in depth. Furthermore you will also learn how to master conversation skills, body language, and emotional intelligence to create more meaningful connections with others.

Read this book through once to understand the concepts and then revisit specific sections as needed. For example, if you need to work on projecting warmth, focus on that chapter. If you struggle with finding things to say, reread the chapter on conversation skills. <u>The key is to practice consistently and make charisma a habit.</u>

Now let's embark on this journey together and unlock your full potential! By the end of this book, you'll have a full understanding of what charisma is, why it's important, and how to cultivate it in your own life. Get ready to transform yourself into a more charismatic and likable person. The world is waiting for you.

CHAPTER 1
WHY CHARISMA MATTERS

Charisma is not just a superficial charm; it's a profound skill that can transform your personal and professional life. Here's why it matters:

Charismatic people often lead fulfilling personal lives. Their ability to connect and build relationships leads to a richer, more satisfying life experience. They tend to be happier because they purposely surround themselves with positive interactions and supportive networks.

Positive relationships are crucial to our mental health and overall happiness.

Charisma can help you build these relationships—in turn making you more likable and influential. People are naturally drawn to those who are charismatic, finding them trustworthy and engaging. This can lead to deeper connections and a more supportive social network.

In the professional world, charisma can set you apart. It's often the charismatic individuals who are remembered, promoted, and given opportunities to lead. Charismatic individuals inspire and motivate others, making them effective in leading teams, projects, or movements. Their ability to communicate vision and enthusiasm can drive collective efforts towards a common goal. Their ability to connect with others and communicate effectively makes them invaluable in any organization. Charisma also enhances your ability to persuade and negotiate. Whether it's closing a deal, convincing a team, or presenting an idea, charismatic individuals often influence better outcomes.

Finally, developing charisma boosts your confidence and self-esteem. As you become more comfortable in social situations and receive positive feedback from others, your self-worth and confidence grow. This newfound confidence doesn't just impact your social interactions; it permeates every aspect of your life. With greater self-assurance, you're more likely to take on challenges, pursue opportunities, and step outside your comfort zone.

Charisma helps you to project an image of confidence, even in situations where you might feel uncertain, which in turn encourages others to respond positively to you. This creates a positive feedback loop: As you receive more validation and affirmation, your confidence continues to build, allowing you to tackle even more ambitious goals. Moreover, increased self-esteem leads to better mental and emotional well-being. **Over time, this growth in confidence can reshape your identity, making you not just more charismatic, but also more resilient, adaptable, and capable.**

Great, so how do we get there?

Mindset

Our journey to becoming more charismatic and likable begins with our mindset. Specifically the beliefs you hold about yourself, the world, and your place in it.

Thoughts are what initiate actions.

Just look at all the amazing things that have been accomplished in our world. The grandest buildings, inventions, and societies all started in the minds of people who challenged themselves to think bigger.

Consider your mindset as the foundation of a house. A weak foundation will lead to a shaky structure, no matter how beautiful the house is. Similarly, without a strong, positive mindset, your efforts to develop charisma will be unstable. <u>Your current results stem from your mindset!</u> Yet most minds are constantly repeating random or meaningless thoughts. Such thoughts ultimately influence your reality. If those thoughts are average, then your reality will be average. If you don't change your mindset, you'll continue to get the same or worse outcomes. Regret and missed opportunities will persist, and the charismatic person you aspire to be will remain out of reach. (JulienHimself, 2023) (Cabane, 2013) (Alux.com, 2023)

"What you think, you become. What you feel, you attract. What you imagine, you create." – *Buddha*

OK, got it, so mindset is important! But how do we improve it? First of all you must **condition your mind for success**. Identify your mindset, beliefs, and attitudes. Are they generally negative or positive? Do you have a growth or a fixed mindset? Like most of us, you probably have an average mindset filled with daily worries and mundane thoughts. <u>Challenge your mind to create better thoughts!</u> Asking better questions is one way to do this. Instead of thinking, "I am not enough," think about how you can be enough or the ways you are already enough. Instead of thinking, "I can't do this," think about how you can do it or about your past successes. Question things and keep exploring in your mind. <u>The answers will come.</u>

Yes, at times thinking positive thoughts can be a challenge. But it's your life and it's ending one day at a time. Thus it's on you to take responsibility for filling your mind with positive, empowering thoughts.

It's on you to make it happen.

Don't let negativity run rampant in your mind! When you find yourself overwhelmed by negative thoughts, repeat a mantra such as "I'm confident, I'm confident, I'm confident" to block out the negativity. Brainwash yourself!

<u>Surround yourself with people who have big ideas</u> and are positively moving forward. The more charismatic you become, the more that interesting

people will come into your life. Remember that great minds discuss ideas, average minds discuss events, and small minds discuss people. Step out and continue to meet new people. Finally, be mindful of what you consume. News, social media and so on are usually filled with useless toxic nonsense. Bad inputs equals bad outputs. Good inputs equals good outputs. Curate your inputs and **constantly fill your mind with positive thoughts.** Start improving your mindset today.

Emotional intelligence

Emotional intelligence (EI) is another critical component of charisma. By understanding and mastering emotions, you can better connect with others and excel in social situations. Overall it enhances your ability to respond appropriately in social situations, which in turn causes people to like you more. Emotions truly are powerful tools for understanding and interacting with others. Managing emotions effectively allows for coherent thinking and better judgment. This is essential for charismatic behavior.

High emotional intelligence promotes better social interactions. It helps in empathizing with others and understanding them. Practicing empathy is crucial for enhancing emotional intelligence and charisma. Try to put yourself in others' shoes and understand their perspectives. Listen actively by focusing entirely on the speaker, showing genuine interest and avoiding interruptions. Reflect on how you would feel in their situation and respond with compassion and understanding.

To further boost your emotional intelligence, engage in exercises that enhance self-awareness and self-management. Inner dialogues, for example, can help you recognize and manage your feelings, a foundational aspect of charisma. One effective exercise is to regularly check in with yourself to identify your current emotions and their triggers. Ask yourself questions like, "What am I feeling right now?" and "What triggered this feeling?" and "Do I need to do some work on the **trigger**"? This practice helps in becoming more aware of your emotional state and understanding the root causes of your emotions. Additionally, maintaining a journal can be a powerful tool for reflection. Write down your thoughts and feelings daily, and review them to identify patterns and areas for improvement. **Reflect on your day and explore how to improve it. Write down your wins and lessons.**

Another valuable exercise is mindfulness meditation, which involves focusing on the present moment without judgment. This practice can help you become more attuned to your emotions and better manage stress. Breathing exercises can also help in calming the mind and maintaining emotional balance in high-pressure situations. This is a detailed subject, but essentially, you have to **learn to calm your mind down** and be in the moment. Begin your journey with some apps to learn the process ("insight app" is quite good for this).

Finally, setting specific goals for emotional development can guide your progress. For instance, you might aim to improve your patience in stressful situations or to express your feelings more openly and honestly. Regularly assess your progress and adjust your strategies as needed. By consistently practicing these exercises, you will boost your emotional intelligence, enhance your charisma, and build stronger, more meaningful connections with others. (Goleman, 2012)

Key takeaways

Understanding Charisma:

- *Charisma is a magnetism that allows you to attract and influence others. It is often perceived as an innate trait, but it can be learned and cultivated.*
- *Charisma can be developed regardless of being introverted or extroverted.*
- *Everyone is born with charisma, but socialization and stigmatization may diminish it over time.*

Mindset:

- *The journey to more charisma begins with mastering your inner world. Thoughts initiate actions, and a positive mindset causes positive outcomes.*
- *Techniques to improve mindset include meditation, affirmations, journaling, asking better questions and surrounding oneself with positive individuals.*

Practical tips

Practice Public Speaking:

- *Join a Speaking Group: Consider joining a group like Toastmasters to practice public speaking in a supportive environment.*

Record Yourself:

- *Practice giving a short speech or presentation, and record yourself. Watch the recording to identify areas for improvement.*

CHAPTER 2
CHARISMA ELEMENTS YOU NEED

In this chapter, we'll explore the elements of charisma in depth. These are subtle yet impactful behaviors and mindset shifts that will significantly enhance your charisma and likability. Additionally, I will highlight the common pitfalls that can make a person seem uncharismatic or even repulsive. I'm sure you don't want to fall into those traps! Therefore, it's essential to <u>trust in and follow the process outlined in this chapter,</u> as it is designed to guide you towards becoming a more charismatic and likable person. This will not only help you learn about what it takes, but will also enable you to utilize it to become more charismatic.

Presence

"Give whatever you are doing and whoever you are with the gift of your attention." – Jim Rohn

We are attracted to people who give us their full attention and presence. Contrary to what many think, charisma is really not about hogging the spotlight but <u>sharing the experience and enjoying</u>

<u>someone else's company as much as they enjoy yours</u>. When you don't enjoy being around other people, they won't want to be around you. When someone is not present they will come across as cold and distracted. When someone is constantly checking their phone or gazing off into the distance, they are being cold and distant. I know the habit can be difficult to break but you must learn to overcome that.

Practice and exposure are the keys.

Utilize presence and engagement to be more charismatic. Whoever is speaking, you or them, be consciously present. Provide the space for a genuine connection and allow people to fully express themselves. It's better to be interested than interesting. **Find things that you like about other people.** Instead of waiting for them to show interest in you, spark the conversation and give them the space to know that you're interested in them. (Marshall, 2020) (Sparks, 2015) (Cabane, 2013)

Listen more than you speak. Charismatic people possess excellent listening skills. A study investigated the effectiveness of active listening compared to advice and simple acknowledgements. Results indicated that participants who received active listening responses felt more understood than those who received advice or simple acknowledgements. Sadly many people make the mistake of zoning out or feeling uncomfortable. They check their phones, break eye contact or get distracted. However you must continually **and intentionally** stay in the moment. This begins with being willing to be present, pay attention, and focus on what the other person is saying. *Weger, H., Castle Bell, G., Minei, E. M., & Robinson, M. C. (2014).*

A crucial part of being a good listener is not interrupting people, even if you have the impulse to do so. **The more you let people talk, the more they will like you.** Please give people your full attention when you interact with them. Create mental images of what they say to help you stay engaged. Mentally repeat everything they say to ensure you listen intently. After someone finishes speaking, wait before you respond. Give them time to say their piece and allow their words to sink in. Show that you genuinely understand what they're saying. People want to feel special and heard and by giving them the chance makes you more likable in their eyes.

"Most people do not listen with the intent to understand; they listen with the intent to reply." – Stephen R. Covey

Fine-tune your attentiveness with meditation and breathing exercises. These practices will help to anchor you in the present moment. If you're impatient, try to calm yourself by staying still. During daily meditations, practice sitting still despite the urge to shift or fidget. Maintaining stillness helps you become more present, powerful, and charismatic. Anchor yourself with your breathing or a particular body sensation, such as rubbing your thumb and index finger together or repeating the word "presence" in your mind.

Warmth

Warmth is the next crucial element of charisma. It is the quality that makes people feel comfortable, valued, and understood in your presence. Being warm and friendly will go a long way toward making

<u>people want to be around you.</u> Warmth can be expressed through your facial expressions, tone of voice, and body language. It's all about showing genuine care and friendliness towards others.

Always try to be as warm and friendly as possible. **Begin with a smile**, one that starts within and reaches all the way up to your eyes. Too many people often have a default negative expression that makes them look cold and intimidating. As such, others may not want to approach them. Alternatively, when you walk around with a slight smile, people are more likely to be attracted to you and reciprocate the same energy.

Another great way to project warmth is to focus on things you like about others. Many of us have a negativity bias and get annoyed by others, thinking they are too loud or annoying for example. Give them a chance to prove you wrong. Try to find things you like about people. Make it a habit to identify three or more positive traits in everyone you encounter throughout the day. When you see people, give them a blessing in your mind. It will put a positive projection onto them and make any future communication smoother. This is similar to the Buddhist practice of metta meditation, which is about developing kind intentions toward others. Such overt goodwill automatically projects warmth.

Additionally, incorporating elements of presence will enhance your warmth. I'm sure you've had the experience of someone gazing off into the distance when you tell them something meaningful. They come off as cold. <u>Don't be that person.</u> Show genuine interest in people. Invest more in conversations by providing detailed answers and statements instead of short, cold replies. Work on giving a little bit extra to the conversations, <u>both in real life and online</u>. (Marshall, 2020) (Cabane, 2013)

Power

Power is the next crucial element of charisma. It's that ineffable quality that allows you to influence and command respect from others. Power can come from various sources, including social status, confidence, expertise, and even the way one presents themself. High-status individuals naturally draw others to them, making them appear more charismatic.

Power and status are crucial elements of charisma.

They create a compelling presence that attracts and engages others. Enhancing your status through confidence, visibility, and displays of success can significantly boost your charismatic appeal. Remember, it's not just about having power but also about how you use it to connect to and inspire those around you.

Think of celebrities and how their presence can captivate an entire room. Their fame and influence gives them an aura of immediately noticeable charisma. High-status individuals are often the center of attention. Their visibility makes them more approachable and noticeable. All of this feeds into enhancing their presence. When someone shows signs of being influential, people naturally gravitate towards them.

Imagine a person in a nightclub holding an expensive bottle of champagne or wine and is surrounded by attractive people. This person displays signs of high status and power, contributing to their charismatic appeal. Their status attracts attention and admiration, reinforcing their charisma in a positive feedback loop.

Displays of power and status can be incredibly inspiring. People are drawn to those who exhibit qualities they aspire to have themselves. Whether it's having a large following on social media, owning a luxury car, or holding a prestigious title, such signs of success influence how people perceive and respond to you.

Popularity is a significant aspect of status. Having many followers or being well-known within a community is social proof of your value and influence. Such popularity can make you seem more charismatic, as people are naturally inclined to trust and admire those with social proof.

Material possessions and appearances also play a role in demonstrating status. For example, having a table at a high-end venue, dressing in designer clothes, or driving an expensive car are all outward signs of power and success. Investing in a few high-quality pieces of clothing can significantly enhance how others perceive you. These displays not only make you feel more confident but also signal to others that you are someone of importance.

Surround yourself with influential and successful people.

Your social circle significantly impacts your perceived status. Become an expert in your field. People respect and admire those who are knowledgeable and skilled. Increase your presence both online and offline. Attend events, engage on social media, and ensure your achievements are visible to others. Position yourself in a high status realm. Whether that's through your career or lifestyle, think carefully on how to achieve status in your life and execute the plan. Maybe it's about living in a new neighborhood, going to a new restaurant or switching careers.

Lastly, don't be afraid to display your accomplishments and successes. Whether it's through social media posts or casual conversations, let others know about your achievements. Go ahead and flex a little! (Cabane, 2013)

Humor

Many of us wonder how to be funnier, especially those of us who are socially anxious or introverted. Fortunately, becoming funny doesn't require much effort but rather an understanding of some fundamental laws of comedy. Just like charisma, humor can be learned and <u>is not solely an innate trait.</u>

Firstly, we have to understand what humor is. Essentially it is a comment or action that gives pleasure, delight, or playfulness. Humor serves as a powerful tool to connect with others, reduce negative emotions and create many positive outcomes. Ultimately, being funny is about providing entertainment and joy to others. Laughter relieves tension, boosts mood, and has numerous health benefits. Really it is a superpower that can break down defenses, foster connections, and even indicate intelligence or savvy.

That's all good to know, but how can you actually make people laugh? And what if you're a bit of a stiff person who is always serious? First of all, **allow**

yourself to be funny. Don't hold back on your sense of humor. Embrace your unique perspectives on life and find comedy in your personal experiences. Even joking about yourself can make others more comfortable and open to laughter. Just be careful not to cross the line into discomfort or being offensive. Try to stay light-hearted.

Share the things you think are funny and observe the reactions. Don't do it expecting a reaction; do it because you think it's funny, and do **that** with conviction. No holding back or being timid about it. That would just come off as awkward. Take a look at some comedians and how they do it. Some get heckled. But many also get huge laughs. Embrace it—without being purposely divisive or controversial. You won't make everyone laugh. But that's not the point anyway. You're being light-hearted in your expression, making everyone more relaxed. Keep humor positive and avoid topics that could be misinterpreted or deemed inappropriate.

Ultimately, what I am trying to get across is to **loosen up**. Being self-conscious and uptight hinders your ability to be funny. Smile and laugh more to create a humorous atmosphere. In summary, here are a few ways you can do that.

- Find humor in everyday life
- Find comedy in personal experiences

- Spend time with funny people
- Learn from comedy shows and stand up comedians

Experiment with different approaches: Try different styles of humor and find what suits your personality. Observe and refine your style based on reactions. Master timing, which enhances comedic delivery. Pause before punchlines to build suspense and allow time for laughter.

Lastly here a few funny strategies:

- Respond with opposite answers: Give surprising responses to yes/no questions to create unexpected humor.
- Play with numbers: Use exaggeration or understatement with numbers to surprise and amuse your audience.

Humor is a skill that can be honed over time By permitting yourself to be funny, embracing your unique perspective, practicing regularly, and understanding your audience, you can develop a natural sense of humor that enhances your charisma. Go ahead, try, and remember to not hold yourself back. (*Charisma, Humour & Confidence—Upgrade Your SOCIAL SKILLS*, n.d.) (Academy, 2024)

Beware the killers of charisma

Now that we know the elements of charisma, we also need to know what kills it. Beware of the following because they might make you repel others!

Neediness

Nobody wants to be around needy people. <u>Constantly remind yourself not to do needy things</u>. Being non-needy means putting your goals, interests, and desires before anyone else's. Lead the way! Invite people to places you want to go, take responsibility for your social life, and fill your calendar with interesting activities. Do **your** thing, express yourself and don't expect people to respond positively.

Have a mission and purpose in life,

whether making more money, becoming more successful in business, or becoming more charismatic. Don't stress about attracting people; it will happen naturally when you express yourself authentically and don't care about the outcome. Think of yourself as a leader. A great leader is responsible; they are not needy and they rarely complain. Take responsibility for everything in your life. This attitude will make you more resilient and charismatic, allowing you to put positive energy into the world without getting jaded.

Finally, achieving financial independence will also make you more charismatic. When you're not reliant on others, you will be less needy. Such self-sufficiency ultimately enhances your charisma. (Sparks, 2015) (Settle, 2016) (Marshall, 2020)

Imposter syndrome

When I used to work as a DJ, it felt like I belonged in the club. People wanted to talk to me. There was no anxiety in me talking to new people either. A common problem for people in high pressure environments and situations is that they feel like they don't belong there. Known as imposter syndrome, one must overcome this spell. Realize that most people don't even notice or think about you. They are too busy thinking about how they look or feel. Remember the joke "wherever you go, there you are"? It's actually quite profound. You're never really an imposter, are you?

Imposter syndrome is a limiting belief. One that can be broken by emotion and experience. Train yourself to feel emotions of empowerment. Imagine that you are the owner of the place you're in. Your life will be better off if you walk around

<u>thinking you are the greatest.</u> That's a fact. When you have that mindset, it will start to change your reality. In turn it will lead to a stack up of experience and emotion to contribute to your charismatic character.

"Don't let fear hold you back. Fear is just a thought, and thoughts can be controlled." – Andrew Tate

Being too serious

These days, too many people are far too serious, making it difficult to relate to them or even want to be around them. This is especially true for young men, who, in the rise of polarity and masculinity, are influenced by messages that push them to work hard and sacrifice everything. While hard work is valuable, people skills are among the top skills you can have, with charisma being the most important.

Being too serious can push people away, particularly in dating. You've probably noticed that women many times choose to be with a guy who may not be as attractive as others but is great at cracking jokes and having a good time. He's not overly serious, and that makes him appealing. He is a social magnet and magnetism is both high status and attractive.

In my own friend group, I have one friend who always has a full social calendar. It's hard to get him alone because he's always got plans with so many people. People want to meet him because he's light-hearted and fun to be around. On the other hand, someone who is dry and serious, with nothing relatable about them, isn't as appealing.

These days, there's so much pressure to succeed and maximize every aspect of life that many people have lost the ability to enjoy the moment. Society tells us to grip life by the throat, never settle, and pour maximum effort into everything we do. But in doing so, we lose sight of the joy that comes from being ourselves and enjoying the present.

Being highly motivated to do something is good, but there's a difference between being serious and being sincere. Seriousness is rigid and full of tension, while sincerity is authentic and flexible. You don't have to win every time or achieve every goal at the expense of who you truly want to be.

It's about finding balance in your life, approaching each task with flexibility and adaptability, and having fun along the way. Life is like a dance—it's not about reaching the end, but about moving to the music as it plays and being in the moment. So, be who you want to be, and let go of who society expects you to be.

Embrace yourself.

Key takeaways

Presence:

- *Presence involves giving your full attention to others, making them feel valued and heard.*
- *It is better to be interested in others than to try to be interesting yourself.*
- *We need to ensure eye contact, attentive listening, refraining from interrupting, and deliberate pausing.*

Warmth:

- *Warmth makes people feel comfortable and valued in your presence.*
- *Express warmth through genuine smiles, positive body language, and focusing on things you like about others.*
- *Engage more deeply in conversations to avoid appearing distant or cold.*

Power:

- *Power involves the ability to influence and command respect. High-status individuals naturally draw others to them, enhancing their charisma.*
- *Power can be demonstrated through confidence, social status, expertise, and material possessions.*
- *Practical ways to enhance status include dressing well, maintaining good grooming, and becoming an expert in your field.*

Humor:

- *Humor is a powerful tool to connect with others and reduce negative emotions.*
- *Being funny can be learned and is not solely an innate trait. Permit yourself to be funny by sharing what you find humorous and observing reactions.*
- *Develop humor by finding comedy in everyday life, learning from funny people, and experimenting with different styles of humor. Master timing to enhance comedic delivery.*

Charisma Killers:

- *Eliminate neediness: Have a purpose in life and eliminate all neediness. Lead.*
- *Overcome imposter syndrome: stack up strong beliefs and emotions to build your charismatic character.*
- *Stop being so serious! Be who you want to be, and let go of who society expects you to be.*

Practical exercises

Active Listening Drill:

- *Engage in a conversation where your primary goal is to listen.*
- *Maintain eye contact, nod, and refrain from interrupting.*
- *After the conversation, summarize what the other person said to ensure you were fully present.*

Smile Practice:

- *Start each day by looking in the mirror and smiling at yourself for one minute.*
- *This helps set a positive tone for the day and makes it easier to share warmth with others.*

Comedy:

- *Watch some comedy shows and stand-up comedians.*
- *Observe their timing and material.*

CHAPTER 3
CHARISMATIC BODY LANGUAGE SECRETS

In 1960, during the first televised U.S. presidential debate, John F. Kennedy made a remarkable first impression. As he faced Richard Nixon, Kennedy's composed demeanor, confident body language, and engaging eye contact captivated millions of viewers. While Nixon appeared tense and less comfortable on camera, Kennedy's charisma shone through.

This iconic moment highlights the powerful role body language plays in shaping our perceptions and influencing social dynamics.

Mastering body language can significantly enhance one's charisma.

In this chapter, we will explore how body language contributes to charisma and the practical techniques to develop it. But before we dive into the specifics, there's something even more crucial to address. You can have excellent body language, but without the following elements, it won't make a difference. So, what are these key elements?

Key Element 1: Fitness

Looking and feeling good is a significant advantage in becoming more charismatic. Not only will it give you a great body, it will also make you feel better about yourself. A study by McAuley and Rudolph (1995) highlights the significant positive impact of regular physical activity on charisma. The study found that by engaging in consistent physical exercise, individuals can enhance their psychological well-being, leading to a more positive self-image. Overall, such improvements contribute to a more charismatic presence. (McAuley & Rudolph, 1995)

Now, this isn't a fitness book. That's an entirely different subject with countless books already dedicated to it! However, it's essential to mention that getting your fitness in check is a foundational step in improving your charisma. If you're carrying a few extra kilos, work on trimming down. If you're on the skinny side, focus on bulking up. Building your stamina and endurance will not only make you look better, it will also boost your self-confidence and energy levels.

Consider joining group workouts or fitness classes. Not only will they help you to get fit, but also provide opportunities to connect with others. In these social settings, you'll have the chance to practice and refine your charismatic skills. Remember, being fit isn't just about health; it's about embodying the vitality and confidence that others find magnetic.

Key Element 2: Fashion

Fashion enhances charisma because it makes you feel and look good. Furthermore, it is known to influence perceptions. Imagine a doctor in a white coat, or someone in a military uniform, or a police officer in uniform. Such outfits display high social status and success. Interestingly, studies conducted in New York found that people were more likely to follow a jaywalker dressed in an expensive suit rather than a person who was dressed casually. Similarly, one Danish manager noted that the more formal his clothing was, the more respect and consideration his opinions received.

Present your best self at all times.

Even when you go to the gym, every moment in public counts. You never know who you might meet! Dress and groom like the top people in your business. This means having excellent hygiene, grooming and clothes. Purchase well-fitting clothes that make you look great. You don't need flashy brand names, just clothes that fit you well, match your skin tone and body type. It's not about one silver bullet but stacking up many little wins. For example, you could have a great shirt, trousers and shoes. However, if you have dirty laces or a few creases in your shirt, these small things can work against you. So, yes, check all those boxes before you're out in public view.

Pay attention to how people react to you. I like to test different outfits by noticing how people react to me. For example, I get more attention when I wear specific shirts, so I adapt my style to include more of those items in my wardrobe. Test what works for you. If possible, go shopping with a member of the opposite sex to get their opinion on what looks attractive on you. Research influencers who look a little similar to you and learn from their style.

In addition to looking good, you should also make sure you're comfortable. Uncomfortable clothing will make you feel awkward—and <u>discomfort is a charisma killer.</u> Strike a balance between comfort and looking good. If you live in hot climates, be mindful of certain colors. Certain colors, such as grays, blues, and greens, show sweat stains more clearly and can make you look scruffy. In cold countries, ensure you're warm enough. Avoid clothing that is itchy or ill-fitting. If it's sunny, wear sunglasses to avoid squinting. <u>Eliminate any physical discomfort in advance</u>. Covering these fundamental bases will help you focus on more important things.

Finally you need to consider noise levels, energy levels and hunger. Ensure you've eaten a portion that is comfortable for you so that you're not distracted by hunger. Brush your teeth and make sure your energy levels are high. If it's late at night, make sure you're well-rested. If it's early morning, ensure you're well-prepared and energized. In summary, be well-fed, well-rested, and prepared for the moment. (Sparks, 2015) (Cabane, 2013) (Marshall, 2020)

Body language

Posture

Great body language begins with great posture! A study by Carney, Cuddy, and Yap (2010) reveals that adopting powerful posture can significantly influence perceptions of leadership and authority. These nonverbal displays not only make you feel better but they also enhance your charismatic presence. (Carney, Cuddy, & Yap, 2010).

Charismatic people never slouch or sit with rounded shoulders. They keep their heads up and look directly at the person they are interacting with. If you tend to slouch, you'll need to practice maintaining good posture. Hold your shoulders back and make sure you're sitting or standing upright. Take up space with your posture and avoid fidgeting or excessive nodding. Place your feet firmly on the ground.

Constantly remind yourself to maintain open, confident, and upright body language. Not only will this make you more charismatic, it will also make you feel better. When slouched over with crossed arms, you'll feel more shy and closed off to others. In contrast, you'll feel good about yourself if you're open, upright, and taking up space. Practice some power postures in front of a mirror. Work on conveying and feeling a powerful confidence.

Next, make sure to breathe properly. Good breathing is a skill that improves your body language. Avoid breathing heavily or shortly; aim for nice, even breaths that rejuvenate and calm your body. Inhale slowly through your nose and exhale through your mouth. If you ever feel anxiety rising, you can use breathing techniques to calm yourself down. Anchoring your state to your breath will help you to become more present, and as a side benefit it will improve your body language.

Facial expressions

Facial expressions are essential for charisma. Charismatic people don't scowl or frown; they usually have a slight smile or a calm look that projects warmth and friendliness. However many people have a default moody look and when they catch someone's eye, it appears they are upset. Ask yourself if you look friendly, warm, and present. Practice having a slight smile on your face. When people catch your eye, it will seem like you're always smiling. This in turn will elicit positive reactions. Moreover, it creates a positive reinforcing cycle, lifting your mood and making you feel much better about yourself.

Practice smiling in front of the mirror each day. See how it lights up your face. Work on maintaining a slight smile all of the time. Do it all the way up to your eyes. Maintain this in your conversations and throughout the day. It will help you to project warmth, which is a vital part of being more charismatic. (Marshall, 2020)

Eye contact

Maintaining effective eye contact is a crucial aspect of engaging communication. However many people avoid eye contact due to shyness or distraction. Unfortunately this will diminish your charisma. Let's get to work on improving our eye contact! During conversations, aim to hold eye contact for about 60-70% of the time to show that you are engaged and interested without being overly intense. It's natural to break eye contact occasionally; you can glance to the side or at something related to the conversation to avoid staring, which can put people off.

In one-on-one settings, maintaining eye contact for about 60-70% of the time is usually appropriate; whereas in group settings, you should shift your gaze to make eye contact with different group members. Break eye contact at natural points in the conversation, such as when you're thinking or emphasizing a point. Try not to stare at particular parts of someone's body, as it might make them self-conscious.

Cultural differences also play an important role in eye-contact norms. In some cultures, prolonged eye contact can be seen as disrespectful, while in others, it is a sign of confidence and attentiveness. Adjust your eye contact according to the situation. In formal settings, slightly less eye contact may be appropriate, whereas in informal or personal settings, more eye contact can help build rapport.

Practicing eye contact with friends or in front of a mirror can help you become more comfortable with it. Ensure your body language is open and relaxed while maintaining eye contact to convey warmth and confidence. Focus on staying present in the conversation, as genuine interest in the other person will naturally lead to appropriate eye contact. By following these guidelines, you can ensure that your eye contact enhances your charisma and helps build strong connections with others. (Cabane, 2013) (Kleinke, 1986). (Kellerman, Lewis, & Laird, 1989)

Vocal power

Many people talk too quietly and then wonder why others don't understand or pay attention to them. Try to <u>project your voice a little bit louder</u>. In doing so you'll notice that people are more engaged when you speak. However, conversely, if you already speak loudly, you might not need to increase your volume.

A slow, measured tempo with frequent pauses is an excellent way to convey confidence. To project more warmth in your voice, smile—again it's really a superpower! Even smiling on the phone makes a difference. (Cabane, 2013).

For added charisma boosts in conversation, try the following quick tips:

- Lower the tone of your voice at the end of your speaking. This simple adjustment can make your speech sound more confident and authoritative.
- Pause before you speak. This brief moment of silence can create anticipation and demonstrate that you are thoughtful in your responses, making you appear more composed and charismatic.

Charismatic body language

Even if you have a great story and a powerful message, weak body language will undermine your charisma. Presence, power, and warmth can all be projected through your body language, giving you a charismatic persona.

Use your hands when you speak, but avoid fidgeting or touching your face too much. Practice this in front of a mirror or observe how others use their hands when they speak. Don't shut yourself off with defensive body language such as crossing your arms. Instead, use open hand gestures and movements. Aim for a warm, charismatic, comfortable, and spacious presence.

Donald Trump is particularly good at conveying his points with hand gestures. Andrew Tate is another example of using hand gestures to emphasize points when he speaks. Watch how these individuals use their hands to add emphasis and practice incorporating similar gestures into your speaking style. Practice hand gestures at home. Read a book in front of a mirror, using your hands to emphasize key points.

Lastly, we can use touch to increase charisma and engagement. A great way to do this is to maintain an arm's distance from the person you're interacting with, and then subtly grab their attention with an occasional light tap on the shoulder or arm. This is relatively intimate but can be effective if done lightly and not too often. (Cabane, 2013) (Charisma, Humour & Confidence - Upgrade Your SOCIAL SKILLS, n.d.) (Marshall, 2020)

Space

Personal space is something you have to intuitively understand and learn from experience. Avoid getting too close when you meet a new person, as this breaks the boundaries of intimacy. A good rule of thumb is to stay about a meter away from anyone you don't know well. If you reach out your hands, you shouldn't be able to touch them without fully extending your arms. That is a good gauge of distance. Anything closer than that is usually reserved for couples or people who know each other very well.

Let me give you an example of violating personal space. I was waiting for a train recently, standing on the platform, when a guy approached me and started talking. He got too close right away, and I had to step back. Then he stepped forward again, so I took another step back. I don't mind talking to strangers, but when strangers invade my personal space, it makes me feel uncomfortable. Eventually, I just said, "Look, man, nice to meet you," and I walked away. (He needs to read this book!)

Whenever you're with a stranger, and you have to be close, turn slightly sideways so you're not directly facing them. Face-to-face proximity can feel confrontational. Many people who lack emotional intelligence fail to understand this. I've been to many networking events where people lean in way too closely, and it repels others. Don't be that person. Develop a good sense of personal space. (Cabane, 2013)

Mirroring

Various studies have proven that mirroring someone's body language can increase connection quality. I've used this technique a few times, including interviews. During a particular interview many years ago, I was one out of 25 candidates interviewed for a job. I used charismatic techniques including mirroring and asking open-ended questions. As a result, I was successfully hired.

Mirroring involves subtly copying the other person's overall posture. For example, you might mimic how they hold their head, place their feet, sit in their chair, or gesture. It's important not to be too obvious about it. Avoid instantly shifting into their exact positions. Instead, be very subtle about your movements. Pay attention to details such as how much they're leaning or how they're gesturing, and mirror those subtly. (Cabane, 2013)

Handshakes

Handshakes are one of the most universally recognized forms of greeting, often serving as a first impression in personal and professional settings. The quality of a handshake can communicate a great deal about a person's confidence, respect, and openness. Understanding the nuances of a proper handshake can significantly enhance your social and professional interactions.

A good handshake improves the quality of the interaction, producing a higher degree of intimacy and trust within seconds. Ensure your hand is not too tight or too loose, as either extreme can create an awkward or uncomfortable experience for the other person. It should be firm but not overpowering. The grip should be strong enough to convey confidence, yet gentle enough to show respect and friendliness.

Typically, a handshake should last about 2-3 seconds, which is long enough to establish a connection without lingering too long and causing discomfort. Two to three pumps of the hand are sufficient, and it's important to match the rhythm and pressure of the other person's handshake to create a harmonious interaction.

<u>Ensure your hands are clean and dry</u>; clammy or sweaty handshakes can be off-putting. If you're aware that your hands tend to sweat, discreetly wiping them before initiating a handshake can prevent awkwardness. Additionally, during times of illness or in situations where physical contact is minimized (such as during a pandemic), it's acceptable to substitute the handshake with a nod, fist bump or verbal greeting. (Cabane, 2013)

Key takeaways

Fitness and Fashion:

- *Being physically fit not only enhances appearance but also boosts self-confidence, contributing to a more charismatic presence.*
- *Fashion influences perceptions of status and success.*
- *Well-fitting, appropriate attire, combined with good grooming habits, can significantly enhance one's charisma.*

Body Language:

- *Good posture, characterized by an upright stance and shoulders back, is essential for projecting charisma. Avoid slouching and practice maintaining good posture.*
- *A slight smile or a calm, friendly expression can project warmth and friendliness.*

- *Understanding and respecting personal space is crucial. Maintain an appropriate distance and avoid invading personal space.*
- *Subtly mirroring the body language of others can increase the quality of connection.*
- *Use hand gestures to emphasize points during conversations.*
- *Light, occasional touches, like tapping on the shoulder, can increase engagement and charisma. However, use touch sparingly and appropriately to avoid discomfort.*

Handshakes:

- *A good handshake is firm but not overpowering, with a grip that conveys confidence and respect. The handshake should last about 2-3 seconds.*
- *Be mindful of cultural differences in handshake norms and ensure hands are clean and dry to avoid discomfort.*

Vocal Power:

- *Use vocal power effectively by maintaining a lower, resonant tone, speaking loudly enough to be heard, and using a slow, measured tempo.*
- *Smiling while speaking can also project warmth.*

Practical exercises

Daily Workout Routine:

- *Improve physical fitness to boost confidence and charisma. Set aside at least 30 minutes each day for exercise. This could be a mix of cardio, strength training, and flexibility exercises.*

Wardrobe Audit:

- *Improve your style to enhance perceptions of charisma. Spend a weekend auditing your wardrobe. Remove clothes that don't fit well or aren't flattering.*
- *Buy new outfits, ensuring they fit well and make you feel confident. Try on each outfit and assess how you feel in them. You should feel great, and nothing less than great!*

Posture Practice:

- *Improve your posture to enhance your body language.*
- *Practice maintaining good posture for at least 10 minutes a day.*
- *Set reminders on your phone to check and correct your posture throughout the day.*

CHAPTER 4
HOW TO TRULY CONNECT WITH OTHERS

Mastering the art of conversation is not just about talking; it's about truly engaging with others, listening actively, and responding thoughtfully. These skills are crucial for captivating people and building deeper relationships. As such they can enrich both your personal and professional life. In this chapter, we will explore conversation skills, which are fundamental to making lasting impressions and fostering meaningful connections.

Charisma is the accelerator that propels average conversations into great ones.

It's the spark that draws people to you, making them feel valued and understood. Whether through the use of engaging humor, being a supportive presence, or knowing how to steer a conversation with ease. Charisma plays a vital role in every interaction.

In this chapter, we'll delve into the techniques and strategies that unlock the door to effective conversation, showing you how to navigate different social situations with confidence and charm. You'll learn how to not only participate in conversations but to elevate them, leaving a lasting impact on everyone you speak with.

Making a great first impression

Every great conversation begins with making a great first impression. This will influence your initial interaction and the ongoing relationship with that person. Therefore it's absolutely essential to do your very best right out of the gate. Think about it, imagine meeting someone who appears scruffy, exhibits poor body language or is obnoxious. You probably won't look forward to future encounters with them. Conversely, you're more likely to engage with someone who is well-dressed, sharp, and charismatic.

People simply feel more comfortable around those who are charismatic.

Entering with energy is a practical way to make a great first impression. Walk in with open body language and a smile. Use expansive gestures and of course shake hands with new people or old friends you haven't seen for awhile. Begin with some small talk to make people comfortable. Use warm, soft eye contact and be present. Keep a smile on your face, especially when you enter a new environment, and always speak through a smile.

Introduce yourself

Social skills are greatly affected by momentum. Before attending a social event, talking to others as soon as possible is vital—especially if you've been working alone all day, because transitioning to a social environment can be quite challenging. You need to get warmed up. Start building momentum immediately by engaging in small interactions. Nod at the security guard, chat with a shopkeeper, or talk with a taxi driver and so on. Upon arriving at the venue, go to the bar, order a drink, and talk to the bartender. This initial engagement will help you to gain positive momentum.

When meeting someone new, introduce yourself confidently with a smile and a firm handshake. Exchange names. You can begin with something like;

Hi, nice to meet you, my name is …

Remember to use the person's name sporadically during the conversation to make it more personal and engaging. You can start by repeating their name back to them when they say it. (Carnegie, 1936)

Nice to meet you …

From here you can get into small talk.

- **Key Point:** <u>Introduce yourself to others at every possible opportunity:</u> at parties, meetings, on airplanes, at work—everywhere. Say pleasant things to strangers; it warms you up and prepares you for the conversation ahead.

How to captivate people

Captivating people in a conversation hinges on showing genuine interest in them. By becoming genuinely interested in other people, you not only win friends but also develop loyalty and deeper connections. As I mentioned earlier, remembering and using a person's name can make interactions more personal and meaningful. Ask open-ended questions that require more than a yes or no answer to encourage conversation. (Carnegie, 1936)

Examples: *"How do you know the host?"* or *"What brings you here today?"* or *"What do you think about [event/topic]?"*

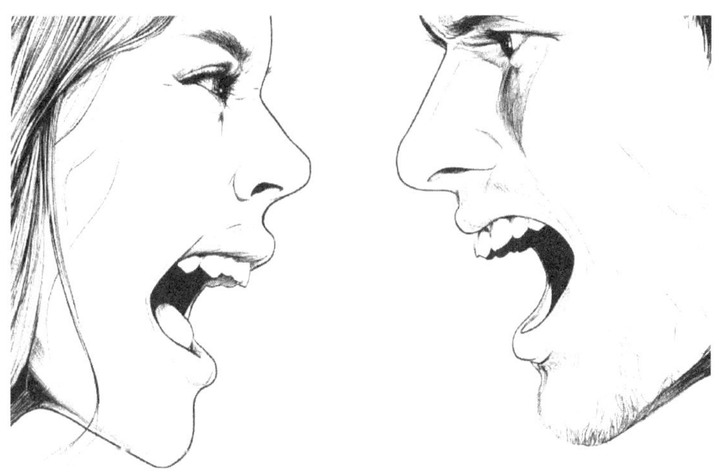

Listen actively and show genuine interest in what the other person is saying.

Nod, make eye contact, and respond appropriately. Explore for shared interests or experiences to build a deeper connection. Mention something you might have in common. For example, the weather, the location, or mutual acquaintances. Offer a bit of information about yourself to keep the conversation balanced.

Example: *"I recently moved to the area, and I'm loving it so far."*

Keep things light and positive. Avoid heavy, political or controversial topics, especially during initial conversations. Focus on positive and neutral subjects like hobbies, travel, or current events. Complimenting something about the other person can be a great icebreaker. Just make sure it's sincere and appropriate.

Example: *"I love your jacket, where did you get it?"*

Lastly, prepare your own topics ahead of time. It will help if either of you runs out of things to say. Keep your prepared topics fairly light. Current events, popular movies, or local happenings are all good choices. Even talking about things in the place that you're currently in. When the conversation is winding down, exit politely.

Example: *"It was great talking to you. I'm going to grab another drink. Enjoy the rest of the event!"*

The more you practice, the more comfortable you'll become. Engage in small talk whenever you have the opportunity to build your skills. By following these tips, you'll be well on your way to making effective and enjoyable small talk in any situation. (Glaser, 2014) (Cabane, 2013)

Go deeper

To build deeper relationships, you'll need to <u>show genuine interest in others</u>. Asking engaging questions can take conversations to a deeper, more meaningful level.

Questions such as:

"How did you get started in this?" or "What brought you here?"

<u>Invite people to share their stories and experiences,</u> so they feel seen and appreciated. Laugh freely at others' jokes to encourage a positive atmosphere. Use light platonic touch and compliments to enhance how others perceive you. Hold eye contact using the tips in the previous chapter. Avoid selective kindness; be universally kind. Refrain from criticizing, condemning, complaining or arguing. Such negativity will damage relationships. Instead focus on understanding and supporting each other. Be a good listener, encourage others to talk about themselves and make them feel important. Don't worry if the conversation goes silent sometimes. Allow it to breathe and allow people time to think.

Mix compliments with playful teasing to create a fun and engaging dynamic. Humor helps build connections. Remember to laugh at yourself to show it's all in fun. It all makes you more relatable and approachable. Being humble and not bragging about your achievements can make a lasting positive impression. Shine the spotlight on others instead of taking all the glory and credit for yourself. Great leaders excel at praising their team for accomplishments, and you should aim to do the same. <u>Humility helps build stronger, more genuine relationships.</u>

Storytelling

Storytelling is a hallmark of charismatic individuals, allowing them to convey messages through engaging narratives rather than just logical points. By framing ideas within stories, you can create emotional connections with your audience. Incidentally this will make your points much more memorable. Stories resonate on a deeper level, as they engage listeners' emotions and imaginations, rather than merely presenting dry facts. Ultimately, this approach helps to forge a stronger bond between the storyteller and the audience. The message is not only more impactful, but also more likely to be remembered.

Effective storytellers excel at weaving multiple storylines together, much like how Marvel movies interlace various plots to create a captivating experience. This ability to connect different elements and perspectives within a single narrative adds complexity and intrigue. To develop this skill, consider some of the most memorable stories from your own life. Reflect on experiences that had a significant impact on you or those around you. Practice telling these stories, focusing on how to integrate various threads to create a cohesive and engaging narrative.

When telling a story, start by capturing your listener's interest with a highlight or a compelling teaser. This initial hook should provide a glimpse of the story's core, sparking curiosity and encouraging the audience to want more. After establishing this interest, delve into the story with emotional depth. Use vivid descriptions, expressive language, and personal reflections to convey the feelings and significance behind the events. The goal is to evoke emotions and make the narrative resonate on a personal level, thereby enhancing its impact and memorability.

Practicing storytelling can greatly enhance your conversational skills. As you become more adept at sharing stories, you'll find that your ability to connect with others, engage them, and leave a lasting impression improves significantly. Storytelling transforms interactions from mere exchanges of information into meaningful and memorable experiences. Truly, it is an invaluable tool for anyone looking to enhance their charisma and communication skills.

Remember, the key to captivating people is genuine interest, engaging storytelling, and a confident, warm demeanor. People may forget what you said and did, but **they will never forget how you made them fee**l. Practice these skills regularly, and they will become a natural part of your communication repertoire, helping you to leave a lasting, positive impression on everyone you meet. (Cabane, 2013) (Marshall, 2020) (Sparks, 2015) (Carnegie, 1936) (Cain, 2012)

Key takeaways

First Impressions:

- *Making a great first impression is crucial as it influences initial interactions and sets the tone for future relationships.*

Effective Introduction Techniques:

- *Introduce yourself confidently with a smile and a firm handshake.*
- *Use the person's name to make the conversation more personal and engaging.*

Building Social Momentum:

- *Engage in small interactions immediately before and upon arriving at a social event to build positive social momentum. This helps ease the transition from solitary work to a social environment.*

Show Genuine Interest in Others:

- *Show genuine interest in others to develop deeper connections.*
- *Remembering and using a person's name can make interactions more meaningful.*
- *Use humor and share emotionally impactful stories to make conversations memorable.*
- *Keep conversations going by actively listening, commenting on surroundings, and allowing silences to breathe. Avoid turning the interaction into an interview. Share your own thoughts and experiences.*
- *Make others feel valued by engaging actively and ensuring everyone feels included in group settings.*

- *Ask engaging, open-ended questions like "How did you get started in this?" to delve deeper into conversations and invite people to share their stories.*

Practical exercises

Small Talk:

- *Engage in small talk with at least three people daily, such as baristas, taxi drivers, or colleagues.*
- *Practice asking open-ended questions like "How did you get started in this?" or "What brought you here?"*
- *Pay attention to the responses you get and adjust your approach based on their engagement level.*

Storytelling Practice:

- *Think of three personal stories that have emotional impact and relevance to common conversational topics.*
- *Rehearse telling these stories in front of a mirror or to a friend, focusing on engaging elements like humor, emotional highs and lows, and vivid descriptions.*
- *Record yourself and review or ask a friend for feedback on your storytelling.*

CHAPTER 5
HOW TO BUILD A POWERFUL NETWORK

Establishing a powerful network is not just a nice-to-have but an **essential aspect of both personal and professional growth.** The happiest and most successful people have strong, close-knit relationships that enrich their lives and reflect their true net worth. A powerful network provides support, opportunities and a deep sense of fulfillment. As the saying goes, "It's not what you know, but who you know." Another adage reminds us, "The best time to plant a tree was 20 years ago; the second best time is today." By starting to build your network now, you'll be taking proactive steps to prepare for future opportunities and challenges. The skills you have learned so far will help to form the foundations of building a powerful network.

This chapter will guide you through the essential steps to create and nurture a powerful network that aligns with your interests, values, and lifestyle. Whether you're an introvert or an extrovert, there are strategies and techniques you can use to connect with others and **build meaningful, lasting relationships**. We'll explore practical tips for becoming a valued member of any social or professional network. By the end of this chapter, you'll have the tools to not only expand your network but to cultivate a circle of influence that supports and enhances your journey towards success.

Where to meet people

Meeting new people can be an exciting and fulfilling experience. However, knowing where to start can sometimes be daunting. But don't worry because I'll show you various places and activities that offer excellent opportunities for making new connections. Whether you are traveling, pursuing fitness goals, attending social events, or simply looking to expand your social circle, there are numerous ways to meet interesting people and build lasting relationships.

Many people make excuses for not meeting new friends, saying they are not an introvert or a "bar person." However, numerous activities and environments cater to different social styles and interests. The key is to research and find events that align with your preferences. Start by asking yourself where you would have fun regardless of meeting anyone? Where are the **types** of people you want to meet?

Friends make friends

Have you ever heard of the six degrees of separation? Essentially it says that every human on the planet is not more than six relationships away from any other person. Your current network or friend group is the best source of new leads. Not only that but it is something you should keep improving.

Everyone has value and all should be treated with absolute respect.

Maintaining existing friendships is just as important as making new ones. Whenever one of your friends asks you out, say yes, even if you feel like staying home. Accepting invites shows enthusiasm and strengthens relationships. Reach out often to your current friends with random texts, funny photos, or interesting articles. Organize events or fun activities to bring people together, such as birthday parties, road trips, or game nights. Inviting people to these events and encouraging them to bring friends along helps you meet new people effortlessly.

Now you also probably have existing co-workers. They too could become personal friends if you bridge the gap between work and personal life. Join lunch invitations or suggest after-work gatherings. Getting to know co-workers outside the work environment allows them to open up and build personal connections. Propose plans for drinks or dinner nearby to make it easy for them to commit.

Go out

Go out to the bars, clubs and restaurants in your area. Find the ones that are popular. Go ahead and make some lists. If no one is free to join you, then go there alone. Going out alone can seem a bit daunting sometimes, but it forces you to connect with other people rather than chatting with your friends. Over time it will get easier. Just say to yourself that you're going for thirty minutes. No one will care. Practice charisma with the staff and the people there. Have a positive mindset, such as

I'm happy to be here and meet new people. Make small talk, ask questions and be positive.

I actually made a huge friend group by going out alone. I simply went out to a club alone and talked with a guy in the queue. He introduced me to his friends, they invited me to an after-party, and then months later I had significantly expanded my network. All from that one conversation! Ultimately it relies on being out and in the present moment. By the way, I have another book all about this.

https://www.amazon.com/dp/B0B9MM85S3

Social and networking events

Attending social and networking events are excellent ways of meeting new people, both professionally and personally. Preparation is the key for successful networking. Understand the purpose of the events you attend and hone your conversation skills using the strategies in this book. Dress well and approach each interaction with humility. Make socializing a regular habit. Consistent practice in initiating and maintaining conversations will enhance your charisma and make you more adept at making lasting, positive impressions on those you meet. It will also give you many opportunities.

<u>Shared interests bring people together</u>. Join social groups related to your hobbies or beliefs. Facebook and other social media platforms are excellent resources for finding and joining groups.

Here are some suggestions:

- **Meetup**: every day of the week there are events going on here. This is mostly in big cities. Otherwise you might have to travel a bit further or move.

- **Facebook groups and events**: the same can be said about Facebook groups and events. Find ones in your local area. Whether it's a group for concert fans, cycling enthusiasts, or brunch lovers. Local Facebook groups allow you to participate in discussions and stay updated on meetups and events. Contribute to these groups and it will help you connect with others and find opportunities to meet in person.

- **Eventbrite**: this is mostly for conferences and specialized events. Branch out and try new things. Remember everyone has value.
- **Mailing lists**: join mailing lists, groups, or pages, and add events to your calendar.
- **Online networks**: these days there are many online paid networks. Browse online and check out what they are about. Research the members and activities. Joining can certainly be worth the price.
- **Local listings:** there are always local listings of trending places. Hop on Google and have a search.
- **Airbnb**: utilize Airbnb experiences to attend tours in your area. You will be with people who have similar interests. Viator and Klook also host tours where you can meet other people.
- **Toastmasters**: join a local Toastmasters club to improve your public speaking skills and meet new people. Many success-driven people will be there and it's a great opportunity to network.

Volunteering and spirituality

Volunteering is an excellent way to meet new people while giving back to the community. There are so many great causes out there. Search in your local area. Go ahead and get involved. SpiritualIty is another positive group activity that often has volunteering opportunities. Furthermore, you can participate in spiritual or religious gatherings to meet people who share your beliefs and values.

Premium living

Living in premium housing, apartments and neighborhoods can offer many opportunities to meet new people. Notice that I mention "premium" because it will attract high-level people. Of course that comes at a price. But it will level up your life. These residences often have communal areas, social events, and amenities that encourage interactions among residents. You might even bump into your next best friend in the elevator! It's all about positioning yourself in the right places.

Fitness and sports

Fitness and sports activities are another great way to meet people who share similar interests in health and wellness. Consider the following options:

- **Gyms**: try attending evening sessions at gyms. It's a busier time and people are more likely to socialize. You can share an exercise machine with someone and make some small talk. By going regularly people will become familiar with you and friendships can grow.
- **Dance**: there are so many styles of dance to choose from. Every city will have regular classes and events. Don't worry about looking like a fool. People will be happy to have you there.
- **Team sports**: team sports naturally bring people together and create a sense of camaraderie. Get involved and build a team.
- **Martial arts**: martial arts not only offers a great workout but also a chance to bond with training partners.
- **Golf**: golf activities often include social elements, such as club memberships and tournaments.
- **Reclub**: explore this platform for finding and joining sports and recreational clubs in

your area. Every day there are packed schedules of many sports.

- **New hobbies**: be open to learn a new hobby or interest, or join a sports team to meet people with similar passions.

Host a meetup

If you have a skill or passion, consider hosting a meetup to share it with others. Websites like Meetup.com or eventbrite allow you to organize local events and attract people interested in your expertise. Whether it's cooking, writing, public speaking, or any other skill, hosting a meetup can bring together a group of like-minded individuals, providing an excellent opportunity to build a social circle. As the event host, you will be the focal point of the gathering, making it easier for people to engage and connect with you.

Miscellaneous

Coworking spaces in big cities provide a professional environment where you can meet other freelancers, entrepreneurs, and remote workers. These spaces often host events and workshops that facilitate networking.

Hostels are a great place to meet new, interesting people, especially when traveling alone. The communal living environment fosters interactions and friendships among travelers from all over the world. Whether you're sharing a dorm room, cooking in the communal kitchen, or participating in hostel-organized activities, you'll find plenty of opportunities to connect with fellow adventurers.

Things to keep in mind

- **Use Social Proof to Your Advantage**: Attending events is just the beginning. To build friendships, you need to engage with people. Make curiosity your goal when meeting new people. Approach groups with the intention of learning one unique thing about each person. This approach reduces anxiety and positions you as a social and friendly person. After making initial connections, circle back to those you found the most interesting.

- **Turn Strangers Into Friends**: To solidify new connections, exchange contact information for future hangouts. Use common interests discussed during your conversation as a basis for making plans. For instance, if you talked about a new restaurant, suggest checking it out together. Hosting events like parties or casual get-togethers can also help you bring your new connections into your social circle. Encourage them to bring their friends, further expanding your network.

- **Friends Don't Make Themselves:** Remember that building a social circle requires proactive effort. Start by setting tangible goals and writing them down. Plan your next gathering, pick events to attend, and set reminders to follow through. Commit to exchanging contact information with every person you speak to for more than three minutes. By holding yourself accountable and taking these steps, you can create opportunities to make new friends and build a powerful network.

- **Invest in relationships:** <u>Continually invest in relationships</u>. This means consistently seeking ways to help others and add value to their lives, not just when it's convenient but as a fundamental approach to every interaction. When you meet people, think beyond the immediate benefits. Consider how you can make a lasting impact on their lives. Offer your time, energy, and expertise generously, without expecting anything in return. By doing so, you create an environment of trust and reciprocity, where people feel genuinely valued and supported. Most of all you appear more likable.

- **Relationships are not transactions:** If someone asks for a favor, do it with enthusiasm and without keeping score. Relationships are not transactions, but investments in mutual growth and support. This generosity and helpfulness will not only strengthen your network but also build lasting, meaningful connections that go beyond superficial interactions.

- **Focus on the quality of time spent with people, not just the quantity:** Cherish the important moments together, showing genuine interest in their well-being and celebrating their successes as if they were your own. Avoid keeping score of favors given or received; instead, embrace the mindset that giving and receiving value is a natural, ongoing process in healthy relationships.

- **Make an effort to stay connected:** Stay in touch even when there's no immediate need. A simple message to check in, a thoughtful gesture, or an invitation to catch up can go a long way in maintaining the strength of your relationships. It's about building a network of trust and mutual support that will not only enhance your personal and professional life but also create a community where everyone can thrive.

Whether you prefer a small group of close friends or a large circle of acquaintances, the strategies outlined in this chapter will help you connect with others and build meaningful relationships. The effort you put into building your social circle will pay off in the form of lasting friendships, personal growth, and a stronger support system. Moreover, it will build your charisma and likability!

Key takeaways

Discover Local Opportunities:

- *Use local resources such as event calendars and social media to find activities that match your interests.*
- *Consider hosting meetups to share your skills and passions with others and attract like-minded individuals.*
- *Joining local Facebook groups also helps you find and participate in events that align with your interests.*

Use Social Proof:

- *Engage with people at events by making curiosity your goal.*
- *Approach groups with the intention of learning something unique about each person, which reduces anxiety and positions you as a friendly individual.*

Exchange Contact Information:

- *To solidify new connections, exchange contact information for future hangouts.*
- *Use common interests discussed during your conversation as a basis for making plans.*

Invest in Relationships:

- *Building a powerful network requires continuous investment in relationships, much like exercising a muscle.*
- *Offer help and add value to others' lives to foster a sense of community and shared success.*
- *Say yes to invitations, reach out often to current friends, and organize events to keep your existing relationships strong.*
- *Building a social circle is vital for your mental well-being, overall happiness and charisma. The effort you put into*

building your social network will result in lasting friendships, personal growth, and a stronger support system.

Quality Over Quantity:

- Focus on the quality of time spent with people, not just the quantity.
- Cherish important moments together and avoid keeping score of favors given and received.

Practical exercises

Event Research and Planning:

- Spend time each week researching local events, classes, and meetups. Use Google, local event calendars, and social media platforms to find activities that interest you.
- Choose at least one event to attend each week.
- Mark it on your calendar and commit to going.

Exchange Contact Information:

- Make it a habit to exchange contact information with at least one new person at each event you attend.
- Follow up within a few days to suggest a future hangout based on common interests discussed.

Say Yes to Invitations:

- For one month, make a commitment to say yes to every social invitation you receive.

CHAPTER 6
UNLEASH YOUR CHARISMA

I mentioned at the start of this book that **real world practice is the key to becoming more charismatic**. By going out and testing what you learn, it will solidify your skills. Additionally you'll need to maintain and improve your charisma throughout your life. It's not enough to practice intensely for a short period of time and then stop. Keep maintaining it, because like any skill, charisma requires consistent effort to stay sharp.

Think about it like this: If you read a book on how to play football, that won't make you a good football player. You must play and use the knowledge you've learned. But playing just once won't make you great!

You need to practice regularly, especially if it's important to you.

Every time you're out and about, you have the opportunity to practice your charisma. Express yourself and make it a habit to start conversations with strangers regularly. When you buy a coffee or go to the supermarket, be charismatic with the people there. If there's an opportunity to speak to someone nearby, take it. Embrace the awkwardness; it doesn't matter how they react. Just do your thing and don't take it personally. <u>Don't expect anything</u>. Just be in the moment, stop overthinking, and be charismatic without needing a specific response. If you practice this daily, you'll naturally become smoother and more charismatic.

<u>Take responsibility for your life</u>. Plan some social time. You've got to be an action-taker and a proactive person. Sitting in front of your TV, playing games, or being on your computer all day is not how charisma is built. It's built in the real world. Of course, you can still work on your business and your health, but you need to divide your life into

important quadrants. If socializing and charisma are important to you, then you have to make time for them. Think of the four burners theory to help manage your time. Imagine a cooking hob with four burners. Each burner represents a part of your life. Health, wealth, relationships, friendships. We can turn some up or down during stages of our life. In this stage turn up the friendships and relationships. (Dodge, 2017)

Now, let me share with you an exercise to jumpstart your charisma!

The 10 X 10 Exercise

The 10 x 10 Exercise is a powerful method designed to help you practice and enhance your charisma. It is a structured approach to breaking down interactions into manageable steps and setting clear targets. Whether you're looking to expand your social circle or enhance your dating life, the 10 x 10 Exercise provides a practical framework to help you succeed.

The plan uses a checklist of 10 boxes for each of the 10 items below. Once you complete a set of 10, move onto the next 10. Aim to complete each set within 10 days. If you fail, go back to the start. There are two versions. One for socializing and one for dating. Here's a breakdown of the steps:

10 X Social

- ***10 Eye Contacts:*** *Make eye contact with 10 people within 10 days. It can be anyone, just take a glance. But don't stare! This simple yet powerful exercise helps you become more comfortable with non-verbal communication. Tick each box once complete.*

- ***10 Opens:*** *Initiate conversations with 10 strangers within 10 days. Start with a simple greeting or a comment to break the ice. Tick each box once complete.*

- ***10 Soft Conversations:*** *Engage in brief conversations that go beyond a simple "hi" within 10 days. Ask questions and make comments to keep the dialogue going. Tick each box once complete.*

- ***10 Venues Alone:*** *Visit 10 new venues by yourself within 10 days. It can be bars, clubs, restaurants, events. But they must be social and busy places. This exercise encourages independence and forces you to interact with others in social settings. Tick each box once complete.*

- ***10 Numbers:*** *Aim to exchange contact information with 10 new people within 10 days. This step is crucial for building your network and following up on initial interactions. Tick each box once complete.*

- ***10 Friends:*** *Form friendships with 10 new individuals within 10 days. To qualify they must meet you for a second time. Focus on building genuine connections that lead to lasting relationships. Tick each box once complete.*

10 X Dating

The dating component of the 10 x 10 Exercise follows a similar structure but focuses on romantic interactions. Here's a breakdown of the steps:

- ***10 Eye Contacts****: Make eye contact with 10 potential romantic interests within 10 days. This will help you gauge interest and build confidence. Tick each box once complete.*

- ***10 Opens****: Initiate conversations with 10 potential dates within 10 days. Use a friendly approach to start the interaction. Tick each box once complete.*

- ***10 Soft Conversations****: Engage in brief conversations that show genuine interest and curiosity about the other person within 10 days. Tick each box once complete.*

- ***10 Venues Alone****: Visit 10 social venues alone to practice meeting new people in a social environment within 10 days. Try to talk with the potential dates there. Tick each box once complete.*

- ***10 Numbers****: Aim to exchange contact information with 10 potential dates within 10 days. Tick each box once complete.*

- ***10 Dates****: Arrange and go on 10 dates within 10 days. Tick each box once complete.*

- ***10 Kisses****: 10 kisses in 10 days! While this goal may seem ambitious, it's about setting high targets to push yourself out of your comfort zone and become more confident. Oh, and by the way it could also be 10 kisses with one person! Tick each box once complete.*

Warming up

Now on some days when you go out to practice the 10 x 10 Exercise it will be difficult to get going. Maybe you've been home all day and it feels awkward. I get it. What you need to do is to get into the right mindset for social interactions. Social calibration and warming up is how you can make it easier. Here are some ideas for warming up before diving into the exercises:

- **Ask for Directions:** Spend 10 minutes asking people for directions. This helps you get comfortable with approaching strangers.
- **Extend Interactions**: Spend the next 10 minutes asking for directions and extending the interaction with statements about the other person and a question or two.
- **Give Compliments**: Spend the next 10 minutes giving compliments to strangers and ending with "have a nice day!" This exercise boosts your confidence and spreads positivity.

That's it! Remember the key to unleashing your charisma is <u>consistent practice and taking action.</u> Load up your spreadsheet and get going in the real world. And remember, charisma is a skill you develop and refine over time. Embrace the journey,

and you'll see significant improvements in your
social interactions and charisma.

CONCLUSION

Charisma is a journey, not a destination!

As we reach the end of this book, it's essential to remember that becoming more charismatic and likable is a continuous adventure. <u>It is not a one-time transformation.</u> Each day offers new opportunities to refine your social skills, connect with others, and build meaningful relationships.

<u>Time is of the essence</u>. I know it's cliché, but life is really short and time flies by. One of the major realizations I've had on this journey is the importance of how we choose to spend our time. A few months ago, I found myself waking up super early to be more productive. Like "monk mode." However I was still ending my days lost in the rabbit hole of YouTube. It dawned on me that those last few hours of my day were not really productive. I realized they could be better spent socializing and building real connections. <u>It's not about the hour you wake up but what you achieve with your waking hours.</u> On my deathbed, I don't want to regret not watching another YouTube video; I'd rather have

memories of deep, meaningful connections with people.

Adjusting my schedule to wake up a bit later and still get my work done allowed me to prioritize social interactions at the end of the day. This shift not only improved my productivity but it has also enriched my life with valuable relationships. Think about it: If you're sad and lonely all the time, then work is much harder. But if you put in time to socialize it makes work easier because your self esteem is higher. The mindset shift is about doing more in less time rather than endless hours of low productivity. On your journey to becoming more charismatic, structure your day well and make time for people. In the grand scheme of things, <u>the connections we make and the relationships we build are far more significant than the content we consume</u>.

Throughout this book, we've explored various aspects of charisma, presence, warmth, power, and humor. We've delved into practical matters, like the 10x10 Exercise, to help you practice and enhance your social skills. These exercises are not just one-time tasks but habits to be developed and maintained. Adjusting your daily schedule to prioritize social interactions, as I did, can be a powerful way to reinforce these habits. By structuring your day to make time for people, you align your actions with the four burners theory, focusing on relationships and friendships during this stage of your life. This approach ensures that you're not just learning about charisma but actively living it.

Remember that charisma is not an innate trait reserved for the extroverted or the naturally confident.

It's a skill that anyone can develop with practice and persistence.

By focusing on your mindset, improving your emotional intelligence, mastering your body language, and engaging in meaningful conversations, you can become the charismatic and likable person you've always wanted to be.

As you go forth, remember that the journey to charisma is about consistent effort and genuine connection. Keep practicing, keep refining, and most importantly, keep connecting. Your life will be richer, your relationships deeper, and your impact on others more profound.

Thank you for joining me on this journey. Now, it's time for you to take these lessons and make them your own.

Embrace your charismatic potential and watch as the world responds to the magnetic, likable person you become!

Wishing you all the best on your charismatic journey,

Darcy Carter

FREE GIFT

Struggling in Social Situations?

Get 5 Quick Fixes to Boost Your Confidence

FREE DOWNLOAD

⬇️ ⬇️ ⬇️

https://subscribepage.com/charisma

REFERENCES

- Academy, L. (2024, April 29). How to be Funnier – Top 19 Practical Tips. Lead Academy. https://lead-academy.org/blog/how-to-be-funnier/

- Alux.com. (2023, March 1). How to improve your charisma [Video]. YouTube. https://www.youtube.com/watch?v=UDyCg8paxhs

- Cabane, O. F. (2013). The charisma myth: How Anyone Can Master the Art and Science of Personal Magnetism. National Geographic Books.

- Charisma. (n.d.). Psychology Today. https://www.psychologytoday.com/us/basics/charisma

- Charisma, Humour & Confidence – Upgrade Your SOCIAL SKILLS. (n.d.). Udemy. https://www.udemy.com/course/charisma-humour-confidence-short-guide-to-social-skills

- Danny Vera. (2023, September 18). Charisma 101: How to be More CHARISMATIC [Video]. YouTube. https://www.youtube.com/watch?v=WPKDt3hFFJQ

- Dodge, N. (2017). Becoming the alpha: Control Internal Energy and Master External Game to Lead a Dominant, Fruitful and Triumphant Life. Createspace Independent Publishing Platform.

- Ferrazzi, K., & Raz, T. (2014). Never eat alone: And Other Secrets to Success, One Relationship at a Time. Penguin UK.

- JulienHimself. (2023, May 23). I spent 17 years improving my CHARISMA. … (My most important lesson) [Video]. YouTube. https://www.youtube.com/watch?v=oQwE4Uhfo44

- Goleman, D. (2012). Emotional intelligence: Why It Can Matter More Than IQ. Bantam.

- King, P. (2019). The art of witty banter: Be Clever, Be Quick, Be Interesting – Create Captivating Conversation. PKCS Media.

- Marshall, G. (2020). Charisma: Conversation Skills, Influence, Social Skills, People Skills.

- **McAuley, E., & Rudolph, D. (1995). Physical activity, aging, and psychological well-being. Journal of Aging and Physical Activity, 3(1), 67-96.**

- Merriam-Webster. (2022). The Merriam-Webster Dictionary. Merriam-Webster.

- Russell Brand. (2020, August 28). How to become CHARISMATIC | Russell Brand [Video]. YouTube. https://www.youtube.com/watch?v=TQmC9VbcC90

- Schwartz, D. J. (1983). The magic of getting what you want. Embassy Books.

- Settle, B. (2016). Persuasion Secrets of the world's most charismatic & influential villains. Createspace Independent Publishing Platform.

- Sparks, N. (2015). As you are: Ignite Your Charisma, Reclaim Your Confidence, Unleash Your Masculinity. CreateSpace.

- (c) Copyright skillsyouneed.com 2011-2024. (n.d.). Charisma and Being Charismatic | SkillsYouNeed. https://www.skillsyouneed.com/ips/charisma.html

- Tuhovsky, I. (2021). 365 Days with Effective Communication: 365 Life-Changing Thoughts on Communication Skills, Social Intelligence, Charisma, Success, and Happiness. Independently Published.

- Weger, H., Castle Bell, G., Minei, E. M., & Robinson, M. C. (2014).

- Howlett, N., Pine, K., Orakçioglu, I., & Fletcher, B. (2013). The influence of clothing on first impressions: Rapid and positive responses to minor changes in male attire. Journal of Fashion Marketing and Management: An International Journal, 17(1), 38-48.

- Carney, D. R., Cuddy, A. J., & Yap, A. J. (2010). Power posing: Brief nonverbal displays affect neuroendocrine levels and risk tolerance. Psychological Science, 21(10), 1363-1368.

- Aiello, J. R. (1987). Human spatial behavior. Handbook of Environmental Psychology, 2, 389-504.

- Hall, E. T. (1966). The Hidden Dimension. Anchor Books.

- Kleinke, C. L. (1986). Gaze and eye contact: A research review. Psychological Bulletin, 100(1), 78-100.

- Kellerman, J., Lewis, J., & Laird, J. D. (1989). Looking and loving: The effects of mutual gaze on feelings of romantic love. Journal of Research in Personality, 23(2), 145-161.

- Abel, M. H., & Kruger, M. L. (2010). Smile intensity in photographs predicts longevity. Psychological Science, 21(4), 542-544.

- Cabane, O. (2013). The Charisma Myth: How Anyone Can Master the Art and Science of Personal Magnetism.

- Cain, S. (2012). Quiet: The Power of Introverts in a World That Can't Stop Talking.

- Carnegie, D. (1936). How to Win Friends and Influence People.

- Glaser, J. (2014). Conversational Intelligence: How Great Leaders Build Trust and Get Extraordinary Results.

- Patterson, K., Grenny, J., Maxfield, D., McMillan, R., & Switzler, A. (2012). Crucial Conversations: Tools for Talking When Stakes Are High.